Poems of Love and Loss

Grieving You

Dr. Michelle V. Boodoo

Author: Dr. Michelle V. Boodoo
Title: Grieving You

Hardcover ISBN: 979-8-218-78364-8
Paperback ISBN: 979-8-218-78365-5
eBook ISBN: 979-8-218-81607-0

IN
HER
NAME

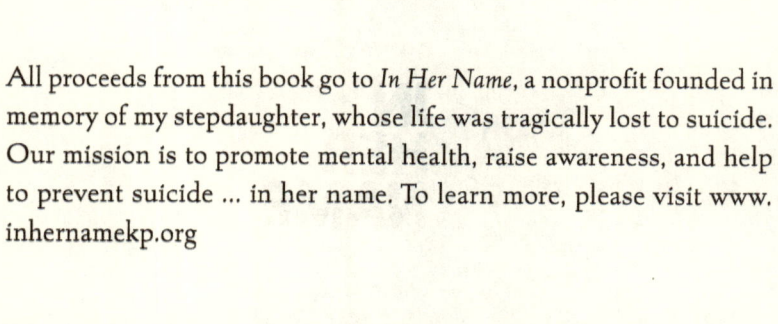

Dedicated to My Beloved Stepdaughter

I Will Always Say Her Name

I will always speak her name aloud,
With love, with pride, forever proud.
She walked this world with gentle grace,
And left her light in every place.

Her name was Kathy, pure and kind,
With a tender heart and a brilliant mind.
She gave her love without a price,
A soul so rare, a soul of light.

She made the darkest moments glow,
With laughter soft or spirits low.
A touch, a smile, a steady hand,
She helped us all to understand.

Though she's gone from earthly view,
Her love still shows in all I do.
This work, this space, this story told,
Keeps Kathy's memory bright and bold.

Author's Note

Dear Friend,

If you're reading this book, it probably means you have known the heartbreak of losing someone you love. First, I want to say, I am so deeply sorry. Grief is heavy, and no one should ever have to walk through it alone.

I began writing after losing my stepdaughter. The waves of grief were overwhelming, and I needed a place to put my love, my pain, and my memories of her. Sometimes the words came to me in dreams. At other times, they arrived in the quiet moments of the day, sitting in the sun, remembering her laughter, or simply missing her presence so much that it hurt to breathe. Writing became my way to stay connected to her, to keep her spirit alive, and to help me survive the days when my heart felt too broken to carry on.

I share these poems with you not as answers to grief, because grief has no simple answers. Instead, I offer them as pieces of my heart and small pockets of love and remembrance of your loved one. I hope that as you read this book, you feel a little less alone in your own grief journey and that you're reminded that love doesn't end, even when life does.

With love and understanding,

Contents

SECTION 1
For You, I Grieve

SECTION 2
For Those Who Grieve

SECTION 3
For Her, I Grieve

SECTION 4
In Her Words

SECTION 5
Photos that Inspired Poems

Introduction

Grief has a way of changing us. It reshapes our days, our thoughts, and even the way we see the world. When we lose someone we love so deeply, there are no perfect words to make the pain disappear. Yet, during times of sorrow, we can still honor their life and keep their memory alive.

This book is a collection of poems born of love, loss, and longing. They came to life in the quiet hours of sleepless nights, sitting in the warmth of the sun, and in moments when my heart overflowed with both sorrow and gratitude. Each word carries pieces of my stepdaughter's essence, and each page reflects the bond that continues beyond her passing.

I hope that as you read these poems, you'll find comfort in knowing you're not alone. Grief is different for everyone, but the love we carry for those we've lost is something we all share. May these words remind you of your own cherished memories, and may they bring you moments of peace, even in the depths of heartache.

This book is not only about loss; it's about love. Love that endures, love that carries us, and love that remains, even when the person we cherish is no longer here.

SECTION 1

For You, I Grieve

These poems are written in the voice of grief itself; the poems are as though they are meant for the one who is gone. They carry longing, love, and the deep pain of absence. They reflect the conversations of the heart that never end, even after someone we love has passed away from this world.

Always Searching

The pain in my heart will always seek,
The sound of your voice, the words you'd speak.
Through quiet nights and skies of blue,
This ache inside still searches for you.

In crowded rooms or a silent space,
I look for remnants of your face.
A laugh, a glance, a fleeting view,
Anything that feels like you.

No passing time can still this flame,
No healing word, no whispered name.
For loss like this, there is no end,
Just love that lingers around each bend.

So, if you feel a breeze drift near,
Or sense a presence drawing near,
That is my heart, still aching through ...
Because it will always search for you.

If Love Could Have Saved You

I reached for the phone to tell you so,
How much you're loved, you'll never know.
But silence answered, cold and still,
A void no words could ever fill.

I know those words can light the dark,
Can warm the soul, ignite a spark.
Yet time slipped past, the moment went,
The call too late, the text unsent.

The "I love you" stayed in my chest,
On that dreadful day, unexpressed.
And now I ache with all my might,
For what I would give to make it right.

If love alone could guard your breath,
You would never walk the road to death.
If love could save, you would still be here,
Living forever ... oh my sweet darling dear.

If You Had Stayed

I often drift to thoughts of you,
And wonder what we would be doing too,
A movie night, your laughter near,
A sunset walk with skies so clear.

Would we cook and dance around the stove,
Or chase new dreams in lands unknown?
Would we plant bright flowers in the spring,
And smile at the joys simple things would bring?

These questions linger in the air,
Moments imagined, rich and rare.
But then the truth begins to shine,
You're not here, though still you're mine.

Like a semicolon in a line,
Your story paused but not decline.
I carry you through all I do,
With love, with memories, pure and true.

You live in laughter, wind, and rain,
In quiet nights and gentle pain.
And though you couldn't stay that day,
Your light, your love, still find its way.

Waves of You

Grief comes in waves, both night and day,
It rises strong, then drifts away.
But in its tide, you softly appear,
Your smile so bright, your voice so near.

The ache is sharp, the tears still fall,
But in those waves, I have it all.
A moment's glance, a sweet hello,
A laugh from times of long ago.

Though pain returns with every tide,
So does your love, right by my side.
And in the sorrow, I find your grace,
A memory of your shining face.

So, let the waves crash where they may,
They bring a part of you every day.
And though you're gone from touch and view,
In grief's deep sea, I still find you.

Birthdays and Holidays

When birthdays and holidays circle near,
I hold you close, my love, my dear.
The ache is real, but so is your light,
Shining from memories warm and bright.

I set a place for you in my heart's space,
And fill it with love that time can't erase.
I laugh at the moments you made me smile,
And let them carry me for a while.

I honor you in the songs I sing,
In flowers I choose, in the joy I bring.
Though my eyes may weep, my soul still knows,
Love like ours forever grows.

So, when these days feel heavy to bear,
I find you in sunlight, in laughter, in prayer.
And even through tears, I celebrate you,
For your love is the gift that always shines through.

The Grief That Never Leaves

Losing you rewrote my soul,
Left behind a shattered whole.
Not just a loss, but a wave so wide,
It pulled the light from deep inside.

It's not just missing who you were,
But how the world now seems a blur.
The laughter changed, the silence grew,
And every hope now carries you.

The questions echo in my mind,
The ifs, the whys, the ties that bind.
They haunt the corners of each day,
Yet still, I speak your name and stay.

I carry grief, but also love,
A bond that storms can't rise above.
So, I remember, speak, and share,
To show the world you once were here.

Your story lives in all I do,
This pain, this love, this ache for you.
And though you're gone, you're never far,
Your memory is where my heart has a scar.

Crushing Weight

Grief is crushing my heart today,
Its heavy hands wouldn't let me sway.
I try to smile, to seem okay,
But tears keep falling and wouldn't obey.

The world moves on, so bright, so fast,
While I'm anchored in the past.
Each breath a struggle, each step a fight,
To make it through another night.

I wear the mask the world will see,
But inside, pain is all of me.
Pretending is hard, the cost is steep,
My dear love, my loss, so deep.

I Celebrate You

Each morning, I feel your presence near,
Your strength and beauty, crystal clear.
Though heaven holds you in its light,
Your love still warms my heart each night.

You guide me gently when I am low,
A steady hand through grief's deep flow.
Your spirit whispers, soft and true,
"I'm still here, watching over you."

I'll celebrate you all my days,
In tender words and heartfelt praise.
My dear love, you'll always be,
A shining part of my life's story.

I Look for You

I look for you in skies of blue,
In every street, in morning dew.
In strangers' smiles, so warm, so true,
I search the world in hopes of you.

I yearn to find in gentle eyes,
A spark of you beneath the skies.
In acts of kindness, soft and bright,
A trace of you comes into sight.

But with each glance, my heart aches,
For nothing else could take your place.
So, I retreat, where memories stay,
And hold you close in every way.

My Grief

Grief arrived in the early dawn,
A silent shadow, never gone.
She stirs my heart with love and pain,
A storm within I can't contain.

She lingers close; she will not part,
A second skin upon my heart.
With every breath, she burns, she stays,
Through endless nights and weary days.

Yet in her weight, a truth I see,
She keeps you, my darling, close to me.
A bond unbroken, strong, and deep,
In love and sorrow, both I keep.

Soft Signs

Every day, I search the skies,
For traces of you in sunrise highs.
In blooming flowers, soft and fair,
I wonder if you linger near.

A passing breeze, a favorite song,
The smell of rain, you feel not gone.
In laughter shared or silence deep,
Your memory stirs from where it sleeps.

I find you in the smallest things,
In quiet thoughts the morning brings.
A shadow cast, a whispered word,
A distant echo barely heard.

Though you're not here in ways I yearn,
In these soft signs, I find your return.
Every day, I search and see,
The love you left still lives in me.

To Honor and Remember

To honor you is how I cope,
A thread of love, a line of hope.
Though you're gone from touch and sight,
Your spirit glows in the softest light.

In stories shared, in candles lit,
In quiet hours where memories sit.
I speak your name, I hum your song,
In doing so, you still belong.

Through acts of love, both big and small,
You live within and guide my all.
A flower placed, a prayer, a sign,
Your legacy and soul entwine.

So, grieve I must, but also live,
And find the strength that you would give.
For when I love and speak your name,
Your light within me stays the same.

When Grief Is Winning

Grief is winning more these days,
Clouding light in subtle ways.
I search for strength, I seek the sun,
But healing feels like it's just begun.

I miss your laugh, your gentle face,
The warmth you brought, your soft embrace.
Each moment now, a silent plea,
For one more glance, one more memory.

I try to mend the shattered part,
The hole you left within my heart.
But some days ache, and tears will fall,
Because your absence says it all.

Yet in the pain, I still hold tight,
To love that echoes in the night.
For though you're gone from mortal view,
Your essence stays near, your love so true.

Writing You Back to Me

When grief feels heavy, cold, and deep,
I write the memories I wish to keep.
Your laughter rings, your smile shines bright,
And warms my heart through the darkest nights.

I write of moments we once shared,
Of silly jokes and how you cared.
Each page becomes a gentle door,
To days I thought I would see no more.

The joy returns with every line,
Your voice, your touch, still somehow mine.
Though time has taken you from view,
The stories keep your spirit true.

And so, I share them, near and far,
To show the world how loved you are.
In every word, you live so true,
Forever loved, my heart holds you.

Your Name

Grief doesn't fade; it learns to stay,
A shadow walking through each day.
But love, it grows and finds its flame,
And so, I'll keep saying your name.

Your light still softly gleams,
It fills my heart and all my dreams.
To speak of you is to keep you near,
To let the world know you were here.

Your story echoes in my voice,
In every memory, in every choice.
To share your truth, your soul, your grace,
It's how I still feel your embrace.

Remembering you is how I cope,
A quiet flame, a sprinkle of hope.
For though you're gone from flesh and frame,
Love lives on when I say your name.

Do You Hear Me?

My heart calls your name in the still of the night,
A whisper wrapped in fading light.
It echoes through the empty air,
And I pause to wonder ... *Are you there?*

I speak in silence, soft and true,
To memories only I can view.
A laugh, a look, the way you'd care,
My soul still feels you everywhere.

I wonder if beyond the skies,
You hear my voice, my quiet cries.
Does love reach where the stars appear?
My heart calls your name ... *And I wonder if you hear.*

I Still Feel You Here

Each day I dream you'll walk back through,
The home we built, the life we knew.
Your laughter lingers in the air,
A gentle warmth that says you're here.

Though they said you were gone that day,
Your love has never slipped away.
In every breeze, in stars that shine,
I feel your spirit close to mine.

And though you cannot come back home,
I never truly walk alone.
For love outlives the deepest pain,
And in my heart, you still remain.

Come Back to
THE NOW

I carry grief from days gone by,
And fear the future drawing near.
Yesterday knocked the breath from me,
Time moved in stillness, painfully.

But in my heart, I hear your voice,
You wouldn't want me to regret my choice.
Not stuck in "what ifs" dark and deep,
But rising from sorrow's endless sleep.

You'd want me here with steady grace,
To keep the light in someone's place.
To do the work, to share the flame,
And help the world in your sweet name.

So, when the weight feels much too loud,
And storms roll in like heavy clouds,
I'll take a breath and softly vow,
To meet this moment and come back to THE NOW.

In the Quiet After

Coping in silence, a storm in my chest,
Grief settled in where love once rest.
The aftermath lingers, raw and unkind,
A weight that sits heavy on the heart and mind.

I trace every memory, soft as a sigh,
Each laugh, each moment, asking why.
But even in sorrow, I find pieces of grace,
In stories I whisper, and photos I place.

Some days I speak your name out loud,
Other days, I wrap myself in a gloomy cloud.
But slowly, gently, I let healing start,
Planting memories of you in the cracks of my heart.

And if my way to remember is mine,
In candles, in flowers, in notes left behind.
Know that I'm trying, day after day,
To honor your life in my own quiet way.

My Gentle Rock

You stood the most powerful and gentle rock I knew,
A beacon of kindness in all you would do.
To every soul, human, creature, or tree,
Your heart whispered softly, *You're safe with me.*

You loved without measure, without any end,
Even to strangers who never could bend.
People and animals, the lost and the untrue,
All found your grace in the light you drew.

Your voice was a lullaby, tender and warm,
A calm in the chaos, a shield from the storm.
Your dream was for a world more loving, more fair,
And you lived each day in the way you'd care.

When shadows grew heavy and the sky turned gray,
Your smile and your laughter would chase them away.
You healed my spirit in ways I cannot name,
Your love was my shelter, my spark, and my flame.

Playful hugs and long talks under the moon,
Moments that ended far, far too soon.
Yet here in my heart you'll forever stay near,
The glue to my soul, the voice I still hear.

So, I walk this journey, though we're far apart,
Carrying you in the depths of my heart.
For you were the sweetest gift life ever gave,
My gentle rock, my hero, my love ... even beyond the grave.

My Heart Calls Your Name

My heart calls your name in the quiet night,
A whisper carried on the moon's light.
I say it soft, I say it loud,
And silence answers through the clouds.

I'm caught in a moment, heavy and real,
Where grief is something I could only feel.
A weight that settles in my chest,
A longing that will not let me rest.

Do you hear me when I cry,
When I speak to the stars in the sky?
Does my love reach where you now stay,
In some far-off, heavenly place?

I hope you know you're still my song,
That I've loved you deeply all along.
And though you're gone from all I see,
I hope you know my love will always be.

My Heart Wants More

Memories are all I have of you,
Soft echoes of a love so true.
They float through time, both sweet and sore,
But still, my heart keeps asking for more.

I see your smile in the morning light,
I hear your laugh in dreams at night.
I hold those moments, etched and worn,
Yet ache for things that can't be born.

No touch, no voice, no warm embrace,
No future days for time to trace.
Just memories that softly pour,
Not what my heart is longing for.

But still, I gather what remains,
The joy, the tears, the silent pains.
Even though you're gone, your love is ever sure,
Memories are all I have, but my heart wants more.

Still Searching

I still look for you in morning light,
In quiet rooms, in stars at night.
Though my mind whispers you're not there,
My heart keeps searching everywhere.

In passing faces, in the breeze,
In rustling leaves and swaying trees,
Grief is loud and strong today,
And all my strength is swept away.

My heart - it aches, it pulls, it yearns,
For what is gone, but still returns,
In memories that gently sting,
In silence, where your laughter rings.

I know I'll never find you here,
Not in the sky or somewhere near.
But still I look, and always will...
Because I love you, and I always will.

The Sound I Miss

My heart yearns to hear your voice again,
A melody lost in the loudest pain.
Soft laughter that once danced in the air,
Now echo in dreams, fragile and rare.

Each day I strain through time and space,
To find your tone, your gentle grace.
A whisper, a word, just something small,
To show me you're near after all.

The silence aches, it fills the room,
Like petals falling far too soon.
Yet in my soul, your song remains,
A love that lives through all the pains.

Three Years Without You

Three years have passed since you slipped away,
Yet the ache feels fresh as that first day.
My heart still wrestles, searching for why,
While grief paints clouds across my sky.

My eyes grow heavy, the tears still flow,
For all the tomorrows I'll never know.
No words can shape this endless pain,
No thoughts can bring you back again.

I wonder what today might have been,
The laughter, the dreams we could've seen.
Instead, I hold the echoes near,
The fragments of you I keep sacred and dear.

With all my heart, I make this vow:
To love you forever, then, and now.
You're stitched into the soul of me,
My darling love, for eternity.

To See Your Face Again

My heart aches with a silent plea,
To see your face, to set me free.
From fading dreams gone after a while,
To feel the light that lived in your smile.

I search the stars, the morning dew,
In every sunset's golden hue.
But shadows fall where warmth once stayed,
And joy retreats where grief now lay.

Your laugh, your eyes, the way you'd shine,
Forever etched in this heart of mine.
No photo, no word could ever replace,
The ache for one more glance of your face.

So, I carry you in every breath,
Through quiet days and nights of death.
And hope, one day, beyond this pain,
I'll see your sweet face again.

Your Beauty Lives On

Your soul was woven bright,
With threads of music, art, and light.
Your poems sang, your paintings gleamed,
Your meals were more than one had dreamed.

Each gift you gave, each work of art,
Was born from love within your heart.
From the first day our paths aligned,
Your joy and laughter became mine.

Through every year, my pride would grow,
As your true colors came to show.
A gentle grace, a spirit rare,
That all could see, and feel, and share.

Though time may change the world we see,
Your beauty still lives on in me.
In every memory, warm and true,
The heart I hold still beats for you.

Your Light I Keep

I want to hold you close and tight,
To chase away the endless night.
To whisper softly, "You're not alone,
Whatever it is, you're coming home."

I would hold your hand and wipe every tear,
Say, "It's okay now; I'm right here."
But sorrow pulls me back again,
To where the silence never ends.

For now, you live in memory's glow,
In all the places love still grows.
My arms are empty, my heart aches deep,
But in my soul, your light I keep.

An Irreplaceable Light

Your presence here was rare and true,
A gift the world received through you.
With every smile, each gentle deed,
You planted love; you made it seeds.

No other soul could take your place,
You left a warmth, time can't erase.
Your kindness wrapped us all in care,
A beacon shining everywhere.

The hearts you touched still feel your glow,
A love that only you could show.
Your essence lingers, pure and bright,
Guiding us softly through day and night.

Carrying On

How do I carry on when the world feels torn,
When each sunrise remind me you're gone?
I search for the strength to face each day,
While my heart aches in its own quiet way.

I hold your memory like a sacred flame,
Whisper your stories, speak your name.
I let the love we shared still guide
Each step I take, though empty inside.

I lean on others when I feel too small,
Let tears fall freely, answering grief's call.
I seek the beauty you would have seen,
In sunsets, in kindness, in fields of green.

Carrying on is not moving past,
It's loving you still, letting that love last.
Though the pain may soften, it will not break,
For my heart walks with you in every step I take.

Hour by Hour

Grief wraps around me, soft and deep,
It guards the place where memories sleep.
Without you here, the days feel slow,
Yet in my heart, your love still glows.

The sunlight falls where you once stood,
I see your smile in every good.
Though tears still rise and blur my view,
They shine because my love is true.

Hour by hour, I walk along,
Your favorite tune is my silent song.
Each gentle breeze, each star above,
Reminds me of your endless love.

How Do I Carry On?

How do I carry on without you here?
This question haunts me, year to year.
I search for answers, some small light,
To soothe my heart through endless night.

You turned 27 ... I see it clear,
Surrounded by those who held you dear.
Candles glowing, wishes made,
Peaceful smiles that never fade.

Would you have felt the hugs so tight,
The love that wrapped you in soft light?
I wonder still, and then I break,
Knowing these dreams of mine, I cannot make.

They wouldn't come true, they never can,
Since life rewrote our precious plan.
And now I sit with all that's gone,
As my heart asks: How to carry on?

I miss you more than words can show,
In every breath, in every high and every low.
But still, your love will lead me through,
As I carry this ache... and carry you.

How Do I Cope?

How do I cope when the dates come near,
When the air feels heavy, thick with tears?
Birthdays, holidays, moments once bright,
Now shadows that ache in the softest light.

I breathe through the waves, let the sorrow be,
And honor your love that still lives in me.
I speak your name, let the memories flow,
For grief and love walk hand in hand ... I know.

I light a candle, I write you a note,
In every small act, my love is wrote.
Though the pain may rise and the days feel long,
I carry you still, you make me strong.

So, I cope by loving you more each year,
By holding you close when you're not here.
And on these days when my heart feels empty,
I remind myself, you're forever a part of me.

I Carry You

My heart will never learn to cope,
To let you go, to give up hope.
It beats, but with a quieter sound,
Since the day you were not around.

I try to walk, to breathe, to be,
But nothing feels quite whole in me.
Each smile I wear, each step I take,
Hides the cracks that loss can make.

Time moves on, but I stay still,
Clinging to the spaces you now fill.
No lesson taught, no healing art,
Can teach your absence to my heart.

So, I carry you in all I do,
Because my heart hurts to live without you.

I Wished You Stayed

The world felt warmer when you were near,
Your voice, like music I still hold dear.
Now the days are quiet, the colors fade,
Oh, how I wish, my love, you stayed.

The stars seem dimmer without your glow,
The rivers are slower, their waters low.
Yet in my heart, your light will not fade,
It shines in the places I wish you stayed.

Through every sunrise, I feel you near,
In whispers of wind, your love is so clear.
Though time moves on, and aches are made,
I carry the hope that you somehow stayed.

One day, I'll see you beyond this shore,
Where tears wouldn't fall, and pain is no more.
Until then, I'll walk the path we made,
Living each step as if you stayed.

Just One Hello

Today I feel so lost, so small,
Caught in a world that doesn't feel whole at all.
I look above with tear-stained eyes,
Wishing you'd come down from the endless skies.

Just one hello, a moment near,
To feel your voice, to know you're here.
A whisper, a breeze, a sign so slight,
To warm the coldness of this night.

The heavens hold what I once knew,
A laugh, a light, a love so true.
And though you're gone, my heart wouldn't let go,
It longs each day for that one hello.

So, if you can, just send a sign,
That you still walk beside my time.
Until the day we meet once more,
I'll keep looking above, my heart still sore.

Lingering

You're always lingering on my mind,
A gentle whisper, time will never leave behind.
In quiet hours or in the rush,
Your memory stirs in every hush.

A laugh, a glance, a breeze that sighs,
You live in echoes that never die.
I find you in the morning light,
And in the stillness of the night.

You walk with me through every day,
Though life has pulled you far away.
Not gone, not lost, just out of view,
But always near, and always true.

No matter what this life has brought,
You're always lingering in my thoughts.

Neverending Love

Grief is relentless; it never fades,
A shadow cast that forever stays.
The pain of losing you runs deep,
In waking hours, and in my sleep.

My heart aches just to see your face,
To hear your voice, to feel your grace.
I long for moments we once knew,
For one more day, one more "I love you."

I want to hug you, to hold you tight,
To keep you safe, to make it right.
And if I could, I would never let go,
But love remains, and so does the sorrow.

Sunshine of My Life

You were my sunshine, pure and bright,
A golden thread in the fabric of light.
Your laughter danced in the morning air,
Your love was gentle, warm, and rare.

In every glance, in every smile,
You made the day feel worth the while.
Your presence bloomed like fields in spring,
A quiet joy in everything.

You were a mirror to beauty's face,
A living poem, a tender grace.
And though you're gone beyond my view,
Your light still shines true and true.

The Language of Grief

Grief is the silent language of the heart,
A whisper of love when we are worlds apart.
It speaks of what eyes can no longer see,
Yet holds what was and what will always be.

A tender echo of moments we knew,
A tribute to love that still feels true.
It lingers in memories, soft and strong,
A quiet reminder of where we belong.

Though you're gone from sight, you're always near,
In every ache, in every tear.
Grief is the love we cannot part,
Forever living in my heart.

Until We Meet Again

Everything I do each day,
Bring thoughts of you along the way.
The smallest thing, the simplest view,
Reminds me how I'm missing you.

I know the heavens hold you near,
Beyond my reach, yet always here.
My heart still aches; it won't let go,
For love still blooms, through all my sorrow.

I dream of when we'll meet once more,
Where time can't part, nor close the door.
A warm embrace, your gentle face,
My soul at peace to feel your grace.

Until that day, my prayers will climb,
Through endless space, beyond all time.
My heart still calls, my soul still longs,
For where you are is where I belong.

What Could've Been

Grieving you is a quiet pain,
A tender hurt I feel again.
A heartbreak wrapped in silent cries,
In dreams that fade as mornings rise.

Today I woke and reached for your sound,
Your voice, I longed to have around.
A gentle laugh, a whispered word,
The sweetest sound I have ever heard.

The ache of all we'll never do,
Clings to the love I hold for you.
And though you're gone, you're always near,
In every tear, in every year.

Some mornings start with empty space,
But still, I search for signs of your face.
What could've been now softly stays,
Inside my heart, through all my days.

When Grief Wins

Grief is winning today,
It crept in slowly, then stole the light away.
Memories of you crash like waves on shore,
Each one gentle but leaving me sore.

I see your laugh, I hear your voice,
In these quiet moments, I have no choice.
The past comes rushing, warm and bright,
While the future fades into aching nights.

I imagine the things we'll never do,
The birthdays missed, looking at the skies so blue.
The late-night talks, the morning calls,
The joy we lost when heaven called.

Today, I sit in what could've been,
In dreams undone, before they begin.
Grief is winning, but only for now,
Because love still lives, and I'll see you soon, somehow.

With All My Heart

As I walk each step through life's winding ways,
I carry you close through my earthly days.
Your laughter still whispers in the morning air,
A reminder of love that's beyond compare.

Through sunshine and shadows, you're always near,
In the quiet of the night, I still feel you here.
Though worlds apart, our souls entwine,
Your spirit forever touching mine.

I hope in the heavens my love finds you still,
Like a gentle embrace that time can't kill.
May you feel each heartbeat, steady and true,
As I live this life carrying you.

And when my journey has reached its end,
We'll meet once more, and my heart will mend.
Until that day, we're never apart,
For I'll carry you always in my beating heart.

Your Life Mattered

Your life was a gift, rare and true,
A light in the world, a blessing in view.
You brought warmth, laughter, and gentle grace,
And left love's imprint in every place.

I wish you had seen through the storm and rain,
The beauty within, beyond all the pain.
I wish you had known in your heart so deep,
The love I held was always yours to keep.

You were valued far more than words can say,
A soul so bright, you guided my way.
The world feels dim without your glow,
But your worth was greater than you could ever know.

Your life mattered, each moment, each part,
And you'll live forever in my heart.

In All I Do

I'll keep your memory in all I do,
In quiet moments and skies so blue.
Though you're gone, your love remains,
A light that softens the saddest pains.

Losing you left a hollow space,
An ache no time could ever erase.
But still, your spirit brings me grace,
In whispered winds, I see your face.

There is no rule, no perfect way,
To honor those who slip away.
Each heart must find its path to cope,
To hold on tight to love and hope.

So, I'll honor you as I know best,
With every breath and every request.
You live in me, you guide me through,
And I'll keep your memory in all I do.

Traces of You

My mind still whispers words to you,
In quiet moments, soft and true.
Each thought, a bridge from me to where,
You drift beyond this earthly air.

My heart still searches, day and night,
For traces of your warmth and light.
Through every crowd, in dreams that stay,
I feel your essence, never far away.

One of Those Days

I'm having one of those quiet days,
Where dreams and memories softly blaze.
I wish my thoughts could bring you near,
To see your smile, to have you here.

In silent rooms, I speak your name,
And hope the wind will do the same.
I close my eyes and see your face,
A gentle light I can't replace.

The world moves on, but I stay still,
My heart obeying love's endless will.
For though you're gone from earth and sight,
Your memory is my guiding light.

So, I hold you close, the one I miss,
In whispered prayers, in moments of bliss.
You live within me, in every part,
Forever carried in my heart.

My Light

You were my dawn, my morning's start,
A steady flame within my heart.
Through joy and sorrow, near or far,
You lit my world like the brightest star.

Though time has passed, your glow remains,
Through memory's warmth and love's sweet pains.
No night too dark, no grief too hard to fight,
You were and still are my guiding light.

The Depth of Love

Losing you opened my eyes,
To love's greatest gifts and its goodbyes.
The deeper we love, the deeper we ache,
A truth the heart can never shake.

Each tear I shed is proof of the way,
Your light still warms me to this day.
It's okay that missing you cuts deep,
For love like ours is ours to keep.

Though pain walks with me, hand in hand,
It's born from a love few would ever understand.
And in that love, you'll always stay,
Forever near, though far away.

Always Searching

No passing time can still this flame,
No healing word, no whispered name.
For loss like this, there is no end,
Just love that lingers around each bend.

If Love Could Have Saved You

If love alone could guard your breath,
You would never walk the road to death.
If love could save, you would still be here,
Living forever ... oh my sweet darling dear.

If You Had Stayed

Would we cook and dance around the stove,
Or chase new dreams in lands unknown?
Would we plant bright flowers in the spring,
And smile at the joys simple things would bring?

Waves of You

Grief comes in waves, both night and day,
It rises strong, then drifts away.
But in its tide, you softly appear,
Your smile so bright, your voice so near.

Birthdays and Holidays

So, when these days feel heavy to bear,
I find you in sunlight, in laughter, in prayer.
And even through tears, I celebrate you,
For your love is the gift that always shines through.

The Grief That Never Leaves

Losing you rewrote my soul,
Left behind a shattered whole.
Not just a loss, but a wave so wide,
It pulled the light from deep inside.

Crushing Weight

The world moves on, so bright, so fast,
While I'm anchored in the past.
Each breath a struggle, each step a fight,
To make it through another night.

I Celebrate You

You guide me gently when I am low,
A steady hand through grief's deep flow.
Your spirit whispers, soft and true,
"I'm still here, watching over you."

I Look for You

I look for you in skies of blue,
In every street, in morning dew.
In strangers' smiles, so warm, so true,
I search the world in hopes of you.

My Grief

Grief arrived in the early dawn,
A silent shadow, never gone.
She stirs my heart with love and pain,
A storm within I can't contain.

Soft Signs

I find you in the smallest things,
In quiet thoughts the morning brings.
A shadow cast, a whispered word,
A distant echo barely heard.

To Honor and Remember

In stories shared, in candles lit,
In quiet hours where memories sit.
I speak your name, I hum your song,
In doing so, you still belong.

When Grief Is Winning

I miss your laugh, your gentle face,
The warmth you brought, your soft embrace.
Each moment now, a silent plea,
For one more glance, one more memory.

Writing You Back to Me

I write of moments we once shared,
Of silly jokes and how you cared.
Each page becomes a gentle door,
To days I thought I would see no more.

Your Name

Your story echoes in my voice,
In every memory, in every choice.
To share your truth, your soul, your grace,
It's how I still feel your embrace.

Do You Hear Me?

I wonder if beyond the skies,
You hear my voice, my quiet cries.
Does love reach where the stars appear?
My heart calls your name … **And I wonder if you hear.**

I Still Feel You Here

Each day I dream you'll walk back through,
The home we built, the life we knew.
Your laughter lingers in the air,
A gentle warmth that says you're here.

Come Back to THE NOW

You'd want me here with steady grace,
To keep the light in someone's place.
To do the work, to share the flame,
And help the world in your sweet name.

In the Quiet After

And if my way to remember is mine,
In candles, in flowers, in notes left behind.
Know that I'm trying, day after day,
To honor your life in my own quiet way.

My Gentle Rock

Playful hugs and long talks under the moon,
Moments that ended far, far too soon.
Yet here in my heart you'll forever stay near,
The glue to my soul, the voice I still hear.

My Heart Calls Your Name

Do you hear me when I cry,
When I speak to the stars in the sky?
Does my love reach where you now stay,
In some far-off, heavenly place?

My Heart Wants More

I see your smile in the morning light,
I hear your laugh in dreams at night.
I hold those moments, etched and worn,
Yet ache for things that can't be born.

Still Searching

My heart - it aches, it pulls, it yearns,
For what is gone, but still returns,
In memories that gently sting,
In silence, where your laughter rings.

The Sound I Miss

The silence aches, it fills the room,
Like petals falling far too soon.
Yet in my soul, your song remains,
A love that lives through all the pains.

Three Years Without You

Three years have passed since you slipped away,
Yet the ache feels fresh as that first day.
My heart still wrestles, searching for why,
While grief paints clouds across my sky.

To See Your Face Again

Your laugh, your eyes, the way you'd shine,
Forever etched in this heart of mine.
No photo, no word could ever replace,
The ache for one more glance of your face.

Your Beauty Lives On

Each gift you gave, each work of art,
Was born from love within your heart.
From the first day our paths aligned,
Your joy and laughter became mine.

Your Light I Keep

For now, you live in memory's glow,
In all the places love still grows.
My arms are empty, my heart aches deep,
But in my soul, your light I keep.

An Irreplaceable Light

Your presence here was rare and true,
A gift the world received through you.
With every smile, each gentle deed,
You planted love; you made it seeds.

Carrying On

I lean on others when I feel too small,
Let tears fall freely, answering grief's call.
I seek the beauty you would have seen,
In sunsets, in kindness, in fields of green.

Hour by Hour

Grief wraps around me, soft and deep,
It guards the place where memories sleep.
Without you here, the days feel slow,
Yet in my heart, your love still glows.

How Do I Carry On?

How do I carry on without you here?
This question haunts me, year to year.
I search for answers, some small light,
To soothe my heart through endless night.

How Do I Cope?

How do I cope when the dates come near,
When the air feels heavy, thick with tears?
Birthdays, holidays, moments once bright,
Now shadows that ache in the softest light.

I Carry You

I try to walk, to breathe, to be,
But nothing feels quite whole in me.
Each smile I wear, each step I take,
Hides the cracks that loss can make.

I Wished You Stayed

The world felt warmer when you were near,
Your voice, like music I still hold dear.
Now the days are quiet, the colors fade,
Oh, how I wish, my love, you stayed.

Just One Hello

The heavens hold what I once knew,
A laugh, a light, a love so true.
And though you're gone, my heart wouldn't let go,
It longs each day for that one hello.

Lingering

A laugh, a glance, a breeze that sighs,
You live in echoes that never die.
I find you in the morning light,
And in the stillness of the night.

Neverending Love

My heart aches just to see your face,
To hear your voice, to feel your grace.
I long for moments we once knew,
For one more day, one more "I love you."

Sunshine of My Life

You were a mirror to beauty's face,
A living poem, a tender grace.
And though you're gone beyond my view,
Your light still shines true and true.

The Language of Grief

Grief is the silent language of the heart,
A whisper of love when we are worlds apart.
It speaks of what eyes can no longer see,
Yet holds what was and what will always be.

Until We Meet Again

Until that day, my prayers will climb,
Through endless space, beyond all time.
My heart still calls, my soul still longs,
For where you are is where I belong.

What Could've Been

Today I woke and reached for your sound,
Your voice, I longed to have around.
A gentle laugh, a whispered word,
The sweetest sound I have ever heard.

When Grief Wins

I imagine the things we'll never do,
The birthdays missed, looking at the skies so blue.
The late-night talks, the morning calls,
The joy we lost when heaven called.

With All My Heart

Through sunshine and shadows, you're always near,
In the quiet of the night, I still feel you here.
Though worlds apart, our souls entwine,
Your spirit forever touching mine.

Your Life Mattered

I wish you had seen through the storm and rain,
The beauty within, beyond all the pain.
I wish you had known in your heart so deep,
The love I held was always yours to keep.

In All I Do

There is no rule, no perfect way,
To honor those who slip away.
Each heart must find its path to cope,
To hold on tight to love and hope.

Traces of You

My mind still whispers words to you,
In quiet moments, soft and true.
Each thought, a bridge from me to where,
You drift beyond this earthly air.

One of Those Days

The world moves on, but I stay still,
My heart obeying love's endless will.
For though you're gone from earth and sight,
Your memory is my guiding light.

My Light

You were my dawn, my morning's start,
A steady flame within my heart.
Through joy and sorrow, near or far,
You lit my world like the brightest star.

The Depth of Love

Losing you opened my eyes,
To love's greatest gifts and its goodbyes.
The deeper we love, the deeper we ache,
A truth the heart can never shake.

YOUR REFLECTIONS

Name of Poem:
Page #

_____

_____

_____

_____

_____

_____

_____

_____

_____

_____

Name of Poem:
Page #

_____

_____

_____

_____

_____

_____

_____

_____

_____

_____

_____

YOUR REFLECTIONS

Name of Poem:
Page #

_____

_____

_____

_____

_____

_____

_____

_____

_____

_____

_____

YOUR REFLECTIONS

Name of Poem:
Page #

_____

_____

_____

_____

_____

_____

_____

_____

_____

_____

_____

YOUR REFLECTIONS

Name of Poem:

Page #

_____

_____

_____

_____

_____

_____

_____

_____

_____

_____

_____

YOUR REFLECTIONS

Name of Poem:
Page #

_____

_____

_____

_____

_____

_____

_____

_____

_____

_____

_____

YOUR REFLECTIONS

Name of Poem:
Page #

_____

_____

_____

_____

_____

_____

_____

_____

_____

_____

_____

YOUR REFLECTIONS

Name of Poem:
Page #

_____

_____

_____

_____

_____

_____

_____

_____

_____

_____

_____

SECTION 2

For Those Who Grieve

Grief is universal, yet deeply personal. This section offers words of comfort and understanding for anyone who is grieving. These poems are meant to be a gentle hand on your shoulder, a reminder that you're not alone in your sorrow, and that love still lingers even in the heaviest moments.

To Those Who Grieve

To all the moms and dads who cry,
To siblings searching in the sky,
To aunts and uncles, friends so true,
And every heart that carries you.

It's okay to feel the waves that rise,
The sudden tears, the aching sighs.
Grief is love that has no end,
A bond that time cannot suspend.

Their memory lives within your soul,
A piece of them that makes you whole.
Each laugh you share, each tear you shed,
Keeps their spirit close, forever in your head.

So, feel it all, both joy and pain,
Remember them in sun or rain.
Make new memories, hold them dear,
For love like that stays forever near.

The River of Grief

Grief is painful, sharp, and deep,
A shadowed path your heart must keep.
It ebbs and flows, yet never fades,
Through sunlit fields and darkened shades.

It lingers softly, it cuts like glass,
A weight that time can never pass.
Though life moves forward, stride by stride,
This ache remains by your side.

Yet, in the sorrow, love still grows,
In every tear, it quietly shows.
For grief is love that has no end,
A timeless rod, you cannot bend.

One Day At a Time

The holidays can weigh so deep,
When memories wake and shadows creep.
A season meant for joy and cheer,
Feels heavy when your loved one isn't here.

Take one day at a time, be still,
Let every feeling have its will.
Your heart may ache, your eyes may weep,
But healing grows in what you keep.

Give yourself grace, release the strain,
It's okay to lean through all the pain.
Reach for a hand, a hug, a friend,
Love holds you close; it will not end.

The Waves of Grief

The waves of grief pull hard and deep,
Through waking hours, they steal your sleep.
A constant tide, they ebb and flow,
Yet never cease, and on they go.

They crash against your fragile shore,
Reminding you of what's no more.
Each wave a whisper, soft yet dark,
A tug that leaves its lasting mark.

Still, in the pull, you find a thread,
A love that lingers, never dead.
Though waves may drag and storms may start,
They cannot sink your aching heart.

The Cure for Grief

We each will walk a different road,
With heavy hearts and aching loads.
No single path can claim what's right,
For healing is born from grief's own night.

Some speak their pain in a gentle tone,
Some write it down when all alone.
Some cry until the tears are through,
Some sit in silence, thinking too.

There is no wrong, no perfect way,
To face the loss that came to stay.
Be kind to yourself, take all your time,
Let patience and love be your lifeline.

Seek helping hands when storms feel near,
From friends, from family, from those who care.
For though it's hard for hearts to believe,
The truest cure for grief ... is to grieve.

Say Their Name

When you say their name, you show you care,
You tell us that their life was rare.
Not just a loss, not just the end,
But once our love, our soul, our friend.

Their name still holds a sacred place,
A glimpse of light, a touch of grace.
You're not reminding us they're gone,
You're proving that their life lives on.

Their laughter, dreams, and kindest ways,
Deserves to echo through our days.
Still loved, still missed, still in the frame,
Their spirit dances in their name.

So, speak it softly, speak it proud,
Amongst the hush, or in the crowd.
It brings us comfort, helps us cope,
A whispered sound of grief and hope.

But tread with care, for hearts are sore,
And some aren't ready to explore.
In heavy moments, grief may sting,
So, offer grace in everything.

Each heart will grieve in its own way,
In silence deep, or words we say.
So, share their name, but share it kind,
With gentle words and love combined.

For in that name, a world remains,
Of memories, of joys and pains.
It's not goodbye, it's how we show,
Their story still has room to grow.

A Lighter Load

I hope today the weight has eased,
That grief steps back, and you can breathe.
May memories drift, warm and true,
Of smiles they gave and smiles from you.

Perhaps you'll hear their laughter's song,
The one that made your heart feel strong.
Or see the twinkle in their eyes,
That mirrored stars in midnight skies.

Let kindness wrap you, soft and near,
And whisper comfort in your ear.
For in each smile they left behind,
Their love still lives, through space and time.

And when the heaviness starts to fade,
May joy return in moments made,
Where grief and love walk hand in hand,
And you remember, and your heart understands.

The Weight of Pretending

They say with time, the pain will fade,
But some deep scars are forever made.
You lose a child, the heart wouldn't mend,
You always break and just pretend.

A smile may hide the silent cries,
While grief still lingers in disguise.
Today, the mask is hard to wear,
The ache too loud, the pain too much to bear.

You feel it press upon your chest,
A sorrow that wouldn't let you rest.
No cure exists, no magic key,
Just tears that fall relentlessly.

Each heart will grieve in its own long way,
In light or dark, in night or day.
In stories told or silence kept,
In memories that must be wept.

So, if today you cannot cope,
Let go of strength and cling to hope.
For even when the skies are grey,
Your love still shines in its own way.

The Weight They Bear

If grief seems strange or hard to see,
Consider this: you've been set free,
From loss so deep, it scars the soul,
And leaves a heart no longer whole.

You have not walked that aching mile,
Where joy feels distant and pain is vile.
Where every smile hides silent cries,
And time can't dim the "whys" and "whys."

For grief has waves that crash unplanned,
It doesn't heed the world's demands.
One scent, one sound, one photo near,
Can bring back love and pain so clear.

So, don't ask why they're hurting still,
Or why tears come fast, or why time stands still.
Just offer grace, a hand, a heart,
Your kindness is the truest part.

Let empathy be how you see,
A soul that grieves eternally.
For love that's lost is never gone,
It lives in those who carry on.

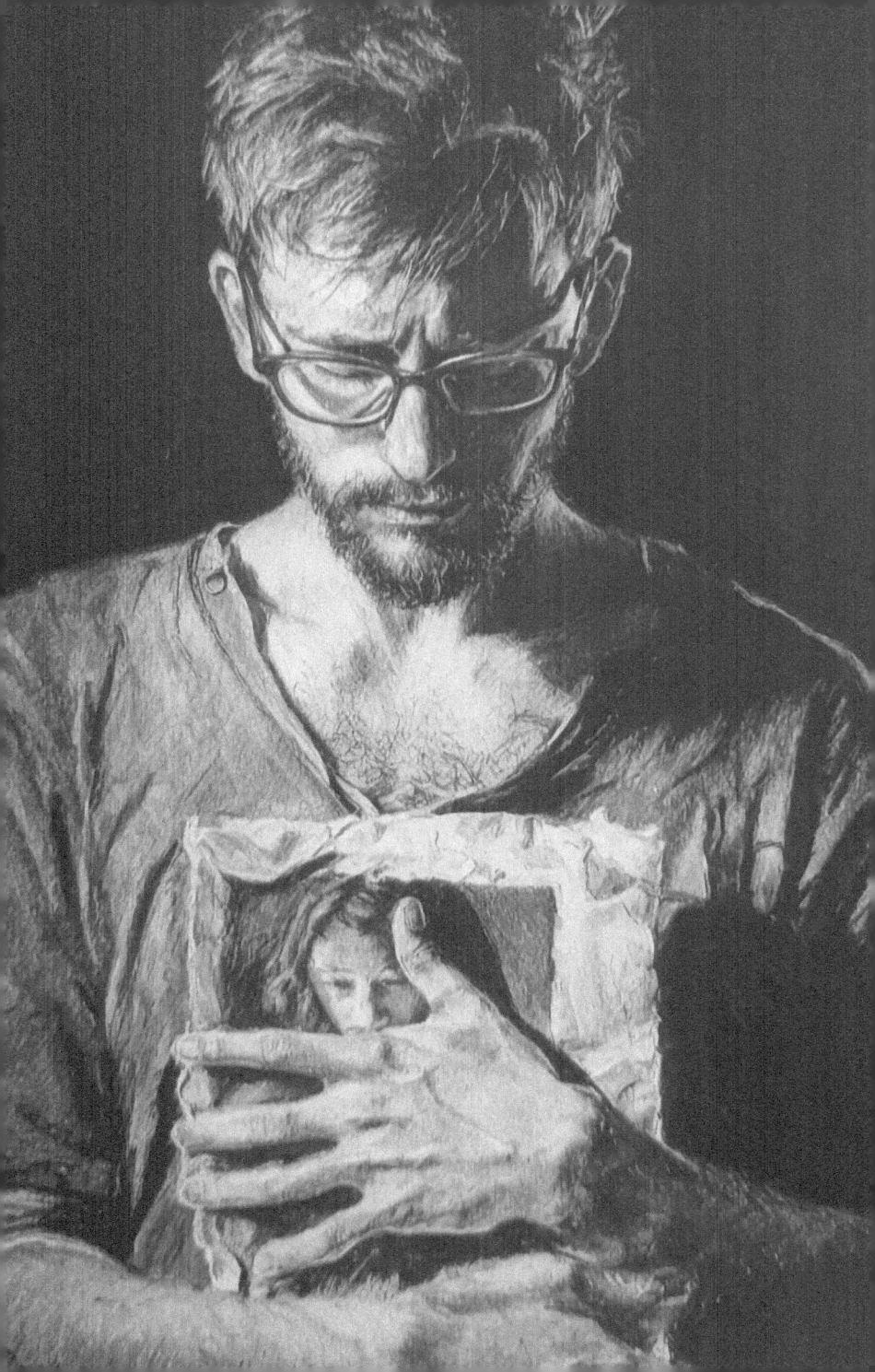

To All the Moms with Grieving Hearts

To every mom whose heart is too heavy to bear,
Whose love still lingers in the empty chair.
To those who hold memories instead of a hand,
Whose dreams were altered by fate's cruel plan.

Your child's light still shines in the love you give,
In the way you teach others how to truly live.
Though your arms may ache for the hug you miss,
Your heart still beats with a love like this.

We'll always honor the strength you show,
The tears you've hidden, the depths you know.
For a mother's bond can never depart,
It lives forever, etched in your heart.

So, here's to you, with love that stays,
Through all the years and all the days.
Though apart you may be,
Your child still loves you... eternally.

To All the Dads with Grieving Hearts

To every dad who knows,
The ache that only a grieving heart shows.
To those who smile while holding the pain,
And carry the love that will always remain.

You've built a world from the strength you keep,
While longing for moments now yours to weep.
Your child's light still shines in the man you are,
A guiding soul, their brightest star.

Though their laughter no longer fills the air,
Your bond is a thread beyond compare.
For love like yours can't fade away,
It lives in your heart every day.

So, here's to you, with love that's true,
From the child who still watches over you.
Though apart you stand,
They're holding your heart in their gentle hand.

In Our Own Ways

A loss will carve a hollow space,
A tender ache time can't erase.
Yet in that space, their love will stay,
A gentle light to guide our way.

No rule can tell us how to keep,
The ones we love, the ones we weep.
For each will choose their sacred art,
To hold them closely in the heart.

Some plant a tree, some write a song,
Some speak their name their whole life long.
Some light a candle, soft and true,
Each flame, a sign of love that grew.

For what we do is ours to own,
A kind of love through grief we have known.
And as we honor them in our own ways,
May their memory warm our darkest days.

The Grieving Ones

To those who grieve and miss their name,
Whose world now feels just not the same,
Hold tight to the love they gave,
Those precious moments, those times we save.

In whispered winds or stars at night,
Their memory still shines so clear and bright.
Though hearts are cracked and full of ache,
Their presence lives in every breath we take.

And if today your soul feels worn,
From carrying love that's bruised and torn,
May healing find you, soft and true,
If only just for a minute or two.

For even shattered hearts still beat,
Still rise again on weary feet.
And love, though touched by grief's own flame,
Still calls them back, by voice, by name.

The Path Through Grief

Grief walks with us, step by step,
A winding road, with tears we've wept.
No two hearts will feel the same,
Each sorrow bears its own soft name.

It's okay to pause, to sit, to breathe,
To gather strength from what still grieves.
To care for self, to gently rest,
It's not a weakness, but a quest.

Let silence be a healing sound,
Find comfort in small things we found.
Reach for those who understand,
Who will sit with you and hold your hand.

Reflect, release, and slowly mend,
Grief has no clear start or end.
But in its shadows, light breaks through,
In peace, in kindness born anew.

So, take your time, no need to race,
Your heart deserves a tender place.
And even on the darkest night,
You'll find your breath, your hope, your light.

Who Do You Call?

Who do you call when your soul feels undone,
When the night wouldn't end, and there's no rising sun,
When the silence is loud and the ache is too deep,
And love once so present now only haunts your sleep?

Who do you call when the memories flood,
When tears drip heavy like blood,
When your heart screams loud for what can't be retrieved,
And you're drowning in all the love you still grieve?

You call on the moments that still hold their face,
The laughter, the light, the warmth, and the grace.
You call on the wind and the stars above,
And wrap yourself gently in the echo of love.

You call on your heart, though it's shattered in two,
For it beats with the memory that still lives in you.
There may be no answer, no cure for the pain,
But in calling out to them, you're honoring all that remains.

To Those Who Grieve

Their memory lives within your soul,
A piece of them that makes you whole.
Each laugh you share, each tear you shed,
Keeps their spirit close, forever in your head.

The River of Grief

Yet, in the sorrow, love still grows,
In every tear, it quietly shows.
For grief is love that has no end,
A timeless rod, you cannot bend.

One Day At a Time

The holidays can weigh so deep,
When memories wake and shadows creep.
A season meant for joy and cheer,
Feels heavy when your loved one isn't here.

The Waves of Grief

The waves of grief pull hard and deep,
Through waking hours, they steal your sleep.
A constant tide, they ebb and flow,
Yet never cease, and on they go.

The Cure for Grief

Seek helping hands when storms feel near,
From friends, from family, from those who care.
For though it's hard for hearts to believe,
The truest cure for grief ... is to grieve.

Say Their Name

Their name still holds a sacred place,
A glimpse of light, a touch of grace.
You're not reminding us they're gone,
You're proving that their life lives on.

A Lighter Load

Let kindness wrap you, soft and near,
And whisper comfort in your ear.
For in each smile they left behind,
Their love still lives, through space and time.

The Weight of Pretending

They say with time, the pain will fade,
But some deep scars are forever made.
You lose a child, the heart wouldn't mend,
You always break and just pretend.

The Weight They Bear

For grief has waves that crash unplanned,
It doesn't heed the world's demands.
One scent, one sound, one photo near,
Can bring back love and pain so clear.

To All the Moms with Grieving Hearts

To every mom whose heart is too heavy to bear,
Whose love still lingers in the empty chair.
To those who hold memories instead of a hand,
Whose dreams were altered by fate's cruel plan.

To All the Dads with Grieving Hearts

To every dad who knows,
The ache that only a grieving heart shows.
To those who smile while holding the pain,
And carry the love that will always remain.

In Our Own Ways

No rule can tell us how to keep,
The ones we love, the ones we weep.
For each will choose their sacred art,
To hold them closely in the heart.

The Grieving Ones

And if today your soul feels worn,
From carrying love that's bruised and torn,
May healing find you, soft and true,
If only just for a minute or two.

The Path Through Grief

It's okay to pause, to sit, to breathe,
To gather strength from what still grieves.
To care for self, to gently rest,
It's not a weakness, but a quest.

Who Do You Call?

You call on your heart, though it's shattered in two,
For it beats with the memory that still lives in you.
There may be no answer, no cure for the pain,
But in calling out to them, you're honoring all that remains.

YOUR REFLECTIONS

Name of Poem:
Page #

_____

_____

_____

_____

_____

_____

_____

_____

_____

_____

_____

YOUR REFLECTIONS

Name of Poem:
Page #

_____

_____

_____

_____

_____

_____

_____

_____

_____

_____

YOUR REFLECTIONS

Name of Poem:
Page #

_____

_____

_____

_____

_____

_____

_____

_____

_____

_____

_____

YOUR REFLECTIONS

Name of Poem:
Page #

_____

_____

_____

_____

_____

_____

_____

_____

_____

_____

_____

SECTION 3

For Her, I Grieve

This part of the book is dedicated solely to Kathy: my step-daughter, my muse, and my eternal inspiration. These poems capture my grief for Kathy, memories of her birthdays, which we continued to honor after her passing, to gifts I made for her, to the countless ways her spirit remains woven into my life. This is where my grief meets my love for Kathy.

Kathy Perez ... Forever 25.

I Will Always Say Her Name

I will always speak her name aloud,
With love, with pride, forever proud.
She walked this world with gentle grace,
And left her light in every place.

Her name was Kathy, pure and kind,
With a tender heart and a brilliant mind.
She gave her love without a price,
A soul so rare, a soul of light.

She made the darkest moments glow,
With laughter soft or spirits low.
A touch, a smile, a steady hand,
She helped us all to understand.

Though she's gone from earthly view,
Her love still shows in all I do.
This work, this space, this story told,
Keeps Kathy's memory bright and bold.

Her kindness flows in every line,
A tribute made with love divine.
And even now, her heart inspires,
She lights my soul; she fuels my fires.

So, I will speak her name each day,
And share the joy she gave away.
For love like hers will never fade,
Through this work, her legacy is made.

One More Talk

I would give the world, the sky, the stars,
To sit with you, no matter how far.
Just one more talk, one moment near,
To quiet your every doubt and every fear.

I miss you more with every day,
Each minute steals my breath away.
It breaks my heart you felt alone,
In battles, no one should fight on their own.

If I could hold you, just once more,
I would wrap you up, down to your core.
I would whisper softly, "You're not alone,
We've got this now; we're solid as stone."

I would take the weight you had to bear,
Split the silence, fill the air
With love so loud it drowns the ache,
I would show you how hearts bend, not break.

But now I hold what can't be touched,
Memories, dreams, and love so much.
And though you're gone, my vow stays true:
I carry your light in all I do.

Never Coming Home

Each day I wait to hear the door,
Your footsteps cross the floor once more.
But silence greets me, sharp and cold,
A story ended, never told.

That phone call broke the midnight air,
I screamed your name in deep despair.
My heart turned heavy, hard as stone,
The breath I knew was not my own.

They said you left this world that night,
Alone, unseen, no one in sight.
The words still echo, sharp with pain,
You're never coming home again.

The years drift slowly past,
Yet every moment seems to last.
For you, my love, my tears will flow,
I cannot bear to let you go.

Forever 25

My grief keeps you close to me,
A tether to your memory.
Sometimes it brings your gentle smile,
And I sit with you... if just for a while.

But often, grief is sharp and deep,
A pain that robs me of my sleep.
It grips my heart, it takes my breath,
A shadow cast by sudden death.

Still, I welcome every wave,
Each ache, each tear, the love it gave.
For grief is all I now can hold,
Of stories past we once told.

You are my light, my heart, my pride,
My love, who never truly died.
Forever 25, yet always near,
In every heartbeat, in every tear.

You left too soon, by your own hand,
A truth I still don't understand.
But love like yours will never fade,
In my grief, your presence always stays.

If You Were Still Here

I lost you to silence, to pain I couldn't see,
And now there's an ache that wouldn't set me free.
My heart hurts in ways I can't explain,
A constant throb, a quiet pain.

My mind is clouded, my vision blurred,
Tears fall for every unspoken word.
I have no answers, no steady ground,
Just echoes of you all around.

I think of today, what it could've been,
If you were still here, if life were kinder then.
The memories haunt, both sweet and near,
Wrapped in sorrow, edged with fear.

But with all my heart, through every year,
I promise to hold you close, my dear.
Though you're gone, you're part of me,
A love that lives eternally.

If Only I Had Known

My grief holds love, it holds pain,
A bittersweet, an endless chain.
Yet in its depths, one question stays,
It follows me through all my days.

How could I miss the weight you bore,
The silent storms, the closing door?
I wish I had seen, I wish I had heard,
The cry for help within your words.

If only I had known your fight,
I would've been your shelter morning, noon, and night.
Though I couldn't change that day we knew,
I'll spend my life loving you.

And in my heart, your light will stay,
Guiding me gently, come what may.

Grief, Why Do You Haunt Me So?

Grief, why do you haunt me so much?
In sadness or even joy, you touch
My shoulders with a heavy hand.
You whisper words I cannot stand.

You punch my gut; you steal my breath,
Then vanish like a breeze in death.
You come uninvited, then drift away,
Yet always find a place to stay.

When will you leave me once and for all?
My body aches beneath your call.
My tears fall endlessly, deep, and wide,
Each one is a storm I cannot hide.

I'm tired of walking through this haze,
Of losing time on foggy days.
I only want to hear her now,
To feel her love, to see her somehow.

Could you just leave, release your hold?
You came when her hands grew cold.
But if you'd leave, just set me free.
Maybe she'd come back to me.

Grief, I beg you, hear my cry,
Let me go or tell me why.
You stayed when she went far away,
And you steal the light from my every day.

Twenty-Five Days with You

The second Christmas felt so cold,
Without your hand for mine to hold.
The lights all shine, the carols play,
But in my heart, joy didn't stay.

Then came a thought, both sweet and true,
An Advent calendar made of you.
Each day a photo, memory's light,
To warm the longest winter night.

I wrote the place, the time, the year,
And all the love I still hold dear.
Each page a gift I long to see,
Reliving what you meant to me.

For twenty-five days, your smile returned,
With every glance, my heart still burned.
Though you're gone, those days revealed,
The love we shared was always real.

Her Daddy's Little Helper

With drills in hand and paint-stained clothes,
Beside her dad was where she chose.
A shovel's weight, a hammer's ring,
Each project felt like everything.

From garden beds in morning sun,
To fences mended, one by one,
They painted walls, they planted seeds,
Met every task, fulfilled every need.

Through sawdust clouds and laughter's sound,
In every task, love would be found.
She learned each skill; she learned it well,
And oh, the stories they would tell.

A yoyo fishing line in play,
Bathroom walls they stripped away,
Each memory etched, each moment true,
A bond that only grew and grew.

Now the tools are quiet, the garden still,
Yet love remains, it always will.
Though she's gone, his heart holds tight,
Her helping hands, her smile so bright.

For her dad, she'll always be,
His partner through each memory,
His princess, now beyond his view,
But building dreams in skies of blue.

The Bond of a Lifetime

One of the purest loves I've known,
Was in the way your heart had shown,
A sister's pride so bright, so true,
In all the things your brother knew.

From days of youth to grown-up years,
Through joy and trials, smiles and tears,
You stood beside him, hand in hand,
A constant light, even in distant lands.

Your eyes would shine with sweet delight,
With every goal he set in sight,
Cheering loudly at every meet,
Your love for him was pure and sweet.

A bond unbroken, sacred, and blessed,
Through every moment, you both knew best,
Your hearts together, always near,
You were the kindest sister ... he loved so dear.

A Birthday Hat

Kathy's 26th Birthday

On your twenty-sixth birthday, we gathered near,
A cupcake, some sweets, your favorites were there.
Cookies and cream, candies and all,
Each one, a whisper of things you enjoyed.

Your dad brought you flowers in vibrant blue,
Each petal speaking his love for you.
And with my hands, I knit,
A birthday hat, a gift your head would fit.

I set it gently on your picture frame,
Lit with the glow of your cherished name.
I thought of Christmas years before,
When I knitted a blanket, you adore.

You called it my hug that held you tight,
Wrapping you safe in the quiet night.
And now you rest on its tender thread,
Still wrapped in the warmth my love has fed.

You can't wear this hat I made,
Yet still, I hope the love conveyed,
And reaches you somewhere, soft and true,
A birthday gift that's always holding you.

Candles in the Rain

Kathy's 27th Birthday

We carried you with every mile,
Up mountain paths, through rain and trial.
The Pyrenees beneath gray skies,
A birthday wish that touched the skies.

The picnic planned with love and care,
Cupcakes, candles, moments rare.
But rain fell soft and wouldn't cease,
So, plans were paused, but not our peace.

That night, beneath a roof so kind,
We dined with strangers, hearts aligned.
A host who served with gentle grace,
Made room for tears we couldn't face.

And when we spoke, the room grew still,
As love and loss began to spill.
Your father rose, voice calm yet true,
"You would be twenty-seven; this walk's for you."

I pulled the candles from my pack,
Still dry and safe despite the track.
An orange stood where cake should be,
A symbol born from memory.

The host approached with flame in hand,
And lit the candles as we planned.
Around the world, they came to sing,
A birthday hymn, a sacred thing.

The following day, with morning's light,
We climbed again, our hearts held tight.
And at a peak so wide and clear,
We shared the orange and shed a tear.

A piece we left for you alone,
Where wind and sky and soul had grown.
Though rain had washed the path that day,
Your light still found its gentle way.

For birthdays come, and some must go,
But love remains in candle-glow.
And through the tears, the miles, the pain,
We'll light your name, in sun or rain.

Forever Her Mimi

It was a warm July evening, two thousand and two,
When a little girl came running, as if she already knew,
That her laughter and smile would forever be mine,
That our hearts would entwine in a love so divine.

Tiny fingers reached out, and without any plan,
She planted herself right next to where I began.
Her soft voice like music, her giggles like art,
And in that one moment, she captured my heart.

I watched her grow, year after year,
A light in my life, a soul pure and clear.
At twenty-five, she was beauty and grace,
The kindest heart, the warmest embrace.

Though she's gone from this earth, her love lingers near,
In every breath, in every memory held dear.
She lives in my soul, in my heart's gentle beat,
My Kathy, my sunshine, my love so complete.

And no matter the time, no matter the sea,
I'll forever be hers, and she'll forever have me.
LOVEUKP ... always, that truth will remain,
For I'll always be her Mimi, and she'll always be my KP.

A String of Beads

I found it tucked away one day,
In a quiet box where memories lay.
Not diamonds bright, nor silver's gleam,
But something sweeter than any dream.

A string of beads, a wooden line,
A little heart, her love's design.
The kind she'd draw with gentle care,
On notes and whispers left to share.

No jewel could shine as true and deep,
As the gift her hands chose for me to keep.
For in this necklace, plain yet rare,
Lives all the kindness she would share.

Now it rests upon my chest,
A priceless treasure, love confessed.
Each bead, a little heart, a story told,
A symbol of her love, worth more than gold.

A Pilgrimage for Kathy

Walking the Camino de Santiago

Beneath the rising sun,
We walked the path you never got to run.
Hundreds of miles beneath a sky so wide,
Through valleys and hills, with you as our guide.

From France to Spain, step after step,
Carrying your love and the tears we've wept.
Pamplona's winds, Zubiri's stony streets,
Echo your name in the rhythm of our feet.

You dreamed of this walk, of distant lands,
Of prayers in silence, of holding our hands.
Though you were not there to lace up your shoes,
We walked for you, in our hearts ... you'll never lose.

No weight too heavy, no climb too steep,
With your memory embedded in the path we keep.
Each sunrise held your brilliant light,
Each star above blessed the night.

For peace, for love, for healing grace,
We walked to feel you in this place.
Kathy, our girl, so deeply missed,
You walked with us still, in spirit and mist.

So, onward we went, through rain and blue skies,
With your laughter carried and love in our eyes.
The pilgrimage was our gift, our vow, our part,
Each step, a whisper from our aching heart.

A Blanket of Love

From nimble hands and gentle grace,
You wove the world at your own pace.
Loops and stitches, row by row,
Turning yarn to love, we would always know.

You taught me: patient, kind, and true,
How needles dance, how colors grew.
That Christmas Eve, my gift was small,
Yet made with heart, it held my love, my pride, my all.

You smiled wide, your eyes so bright,
Ribbons falling in the night.
You wrapped yourself without delay,
And in that moment, I knew you loved your blanket ... yeah!

Wrapped in warmth, each night's embrace,
A piece of me in every knitted space.
You said it felt just like my hug,
A steady, soft, unending tug.

And when the time had come for you to rest,
We wrapped you in what you loved best.
May you feel through every thread,
My love still lingers where you bed.

Forever hugged, forever near,
My heart is in every stitch, my love, my dear.

Flowers For Kathy

Each week, I gather flowers with care,
From garden paths and morning air.
A ritual soft, a sacred chore,
For the one I'll miss forevermore.

I place them gently in a vase,
Wishing for your warm embrace.
The way you smiled, the light you gave,
Still lingers here, beyond the grave.

Before you left, my camera knew
The joy you carried, pure and true.
And now I capture petals bright,
In honor of your love and light.

Though you're gone from my embrace,
These flowers bloom with your gentle grace.
A quiet way to say, "You are near."
Each photo whispers, *Kathy's here.*

I etched your name upon my skin,
A quiet mark, a voice within.
Your initials, bold and true,
A semicolon, meaning too.

It speaks of pain, of battles fought,
Of every tear, of every thought.
But more than that, it speaks of grace,
Of love that time cannot erase.

This ink, it lives beneath my sleeve,
A vow to give, a vow to grieve.
To carry on the light you gave,
To help the hurting, to be brave.

Through every word, through every deed,
I plant your legacy like a seed.
Your story paused, but not the end,
It blooms again through hands that mend.

In Her Name, I rise each day,
A little stronger, come what may.
For though you're gone, your love remains,
Alive in ink, in hope, in change.

A Degree

You dreamed of books, of halls, of lights,
Of knowledge blooming, wide and bright.
Each lesson learned, each goal in view,
A journey you followed and pursued.

Though the heavens called you far too soon,
Your dreams still lingered, like a tune.
Two years had passed, yet still I prayed,
Your work, your time, be not betrayed.

One day, a package, sealed with care,
Arrived quietly, waiting there.
I opened it, my heart took flight,
A gift for you, pure and right.

Your name engraved, your journey told,
A paper crowned in heartfelt gold.
The school had given more than they knew,
A piece of your dream, now alive and true.

On that day, my heart swelled high,
With pride that reached the sky.
For my love above, this gift remains,
A treasured degree that has your name.

My Inspiration

Strong in mind, yet soft of heart,
You bore your burdens far apart.
In silence kept your deepest cries,
To shield us all from tear-stained eyes.

A little giant, fierce and true,
You carried a weight none ever knew.
I longed to guard and keep you near,
To be your shield from pain and fear.

But grief has carved another way,
Your light still guides me day by day.
In life, you shaped my every dream,
In death, your glow is a constant beam.

Forever royal in my eyes,
A princess now beyond the skies.
Through every heart I help and mend,
Your love will live; you have no end.

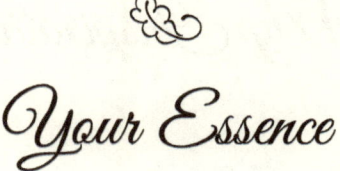

Your Essence

There are days I question, in quiet despair,
If my work in your name is reaching out there.
If the ripples I cast fade into the deep,
Or if your light touches the souls who weep.

Then the universe whispers, soft yet profound,
A message, a story, a voice that I found.
A heart once breaking, now learning to cope,
A spirit once fading, now holding to hope.

In those sacred moments, I see it so clear,
Your love still flows, though you're not here.
I am honored to say with tears in my eyes,
Your essence and love are still alive.

I Will Always Say Her Name

Her name was Kathy, pure and kind,
With a tender heart and a brilliant mind.
She gave her love without a price,
A soul so rare, a soul of light.

One More Talk

I would take the weight you had to bear,
Split the silence, fill the air
With love so loud it drowns the ache,
I would show you how hearts bend, not break.

Never Coming Home

That phone call broke the midnight air,
I screamed your name in deep despair.
My heart turned heavy, hard as stone,
The breath I knew was not my own.

Forever 25

My grief keeps you close to me,
A tether to your memory.
Sometimes it brings your gentle smile,
And I sit with you... if just for a while.

If You Were Still Here

I lost you to silence, to pain I couldn't see,
And now there's an ache that wouldn't set me free.
My heart hurts in ways I can't explain,
A constant throb, a quiet pain.

If Only I Had Known

How could I miss the weight you bore,
The silent storms, the closing door?
I wish I had seen, I wish I had heard,
The cry for help within your words.

Grief, Why Do You Haunt Me So?

When will you leave me once and for all?
My body aches beneath your call.
My tears fall endlessly, deep, and wide,
Each one is a storm I cannot hide.

Twenty-Five Days with You

I wrote the place, the time, the year,
And all the love I still hold dear.
Each page a gift I long to see,
Reliving what you meant to me.

Her Daddy's Little Helper

For her dad, she'll always be,
His partner through each memory,
His princess, now beyond his view,
But building dreams in skies of blue.

The Bond of a Lifetime

A bond unbroken, sacred, and blessed,
Through every moment, you both knew best,
Your hearts together, always near,
You were the kindest sister ... he loved so dear.

A Birthday Hat

Kathy's 26th Birthday

On your twenty-sixth birthday, we gathered near,
A cupcake, some sweets, your favorites were there.
Cookies and cream, candies and all,
Each one, a whisper of things you enjoyed.

Candles in the Rain

Kathy's 27th Birthday

The picnic planned with love and care,
Cupcakes, candles, moments rare.
But rain fell soft and wouldn't cease,
So, plans were paused, but not our peace.

Forever Her Mimi

I watched her grow, year after year,
A light in my life, a soul pure and clear.
At twenty-five, she was beauty and grace,
The kindest heart, the warmest embrace.

A String of Beads

No jewel could shine as true and deep,
As the gift her hands chose for me to keep.
For in this necklace, plain yet rare,
Lives all the kindness she would share.

A Pilgrimage for Kathy

For peace, for love, for healing grace,
We walked to feel you in this place.
Kathy, our girl, so deeply missed,
You walked with us still, in spirit and mist.

A Blanket of Love

You taught me: patient, kind, and true,
How needles dance, how colors grew.
That Christmas Eve, my gift was small,
Yet made with heart, it held my love, my pride, my all.

Flowers For Kathy

Each week, I gather flowers with care,
From garden paths and morning air.
A ritual soft, a sacred chore,
For the one I'll miss forevermore.

KP;

In Her Name, I rise each day,
A little stronger, come what may.
For though you're gone, your love remains,
Alive in ink, in hope, in change.

A Degree

On that day, my heart swelled high,
With pride that reached the sky.
For my love above, this gift remains,
A treasured degree that has your name.

My Inspiration

Strong in mind, yet soft of heart,
You bore your burdens far apart.
In silence kept your deepest cries,
To shield us all from tear-stained eyes.

Your Essence

In those sacred moments, I see it so clear,
Your love still flows, though you're not here.
I am honored to say with tears in my eyes,
Your essence and love are still alive.

YOUR REFLECTIONS

Name of Poem:
Page #

_____

_____

_____

_____

_____

_____

_____

_____

_____

_____

_____

YOUR REFLECTIONS

Name of Poem:
Page #

_____

_____

_____

_____

_____

_____

_____

_____

_____

_____

YOUR REFLECTIONS

Name of Poem:
Page #

_____

_____

_____

_____

_____

_____

_____

_____

_____

_____

_____

YOUR REFLECTIONS

Name of Poem:
Page #

_____

_____

_____

_____

_____

_____

_____

_____

_____

_____

_____

SECTION 4

In Her Words

Here, Kathy's own voice takes the stage. These two poems, which she wrote as a teenager, are pieces of her heart and creativity that I discovered after she passed away. Her words are full of imagination, beauty, and depth, and they remind me (and now you) of the unique light she carried into this world.

Poetry was something she and I often enjoyed. We would sit in the backyard, reading poems and trying to unravel their meaning. At other times, we would make up our own poems by choosing a single word or creating a small scenario, then turning it into verses. Kathy always amazed me with her imagination, her creativity, and her ability to capture so much in just a few lines.

As these poems came to life in this book, I often felt Kathy's presence beside me, guiding me. She will forever be my muse, inspiring not only these pages, but everything I do.

Home

by Kathy Perez

The golden warmth of the universe's heart rays down
Piercing through the floorboards.
The dust mites lay in wait of the dance
they play when wind beacons.
Whispers reign in through the cracks in the window.
The silk air brushed alongside leather shoes,
Fighting with the cold flames of dying embers,
Breathing life into the once desolate and abandoned structure,
Cracking and pounding, the wood settles into a new position.
Old was this place, and alone.
But, no!
A body has claimed this.
Walking with leisure through the rotten halls, singing,
A new home have I, a new home.

Flowers

by Kathy Perez

Pink little petals shivering together as the wind moves across
     the field.
It glances here and there at a particular grouping of blooms,
     making them sway to its rhythm.
It wanted to dance freely.
So, it swayed and beckoned the grass to join.
The flower petals, tired and restless, tear themselves away from
     their stems to be gently cradled to the ground.
The wind then moves further up into the sky to remove itself
     from them, so as not to be a bother.
"Higher, and higher!" it tells itself, aiming for the distant clouds
     above.
Yet it does not reach.
It is limited by the atmosphere to remain where it is, far below
     the milky clouds.
But it does not fret.

It simply resigns itself, traveling to a nearby tree where it is
  welcomed with warm, shaky limbs.
The tree openly dances with this wind, the leaves crafting a
  tender laugh that travels throughout the entire meadow.
Further out into the field lay a lamb and a dog.
They lay side by side on the grass.
The sun is their blanket.
The lamb and the dog are sleeping.
The dog has worked hard, hunting mice and chasing geese for
  the human man and wife.
The lamb lay silent and solemn.
Then gold enters the sky and melts in the air; the sun is begin-
  ning to rest.

Home

by Kathy Perez

Old was this place, and alone.
But, no!
A body has claimed this.
Walking with leisure through the rotten halls, singing,
A new home have I, a new home.

Flowers

by Kathy Perez

Pink little petals shivering together as the wind moves across the field.
It glances here and there at a particular grouping of blooms,
making them sway to its rhythm.
It wanted to dance freely.

YOUR REFLECTIONS

Name of Poem:
Page #

_____

_____

_____

_____

_____

_____

_____

_____

_____

_____

_____

SECTION 5

Photos that Inspired Poems

In this section, you'll find photos that inspired ten of the poems in this book. Each image holds a piece of Kathy's memory. They honor her love, her light, and the beautiful person she was. You'll also find a few lines from the poems they inspired, woven together with the memories they hold. These images are not just pictures; they are reflections of remembrance, celebration, and love that continue even after loss.

My hope is that, as you look through the photos, they inspire you to find comfort in celebrating your beloved ones you hold dear as you navigate your journey through grief.

Moments Transformed into Poems

After reviewing the photos, I encourage you to revisit each poem; together, they may reveal layers of meaning you hadn't seen before.

Her Daddy's Little Helper

"With drills in hand and paint-stained clothes,
Beside her dad was where she chose.
A shovel's weight, a hammer's ring,
Each project felt like everything."

A Birthday Hat

Kathy's 26th Birthday

"On your twenty-sixth birthday, we gathered near,
A cupcake, some sweets, your favorites were there.
Cookies and cream, candies and all,
Each one, a whisper of things you enjoyed.

Your dad brought you flowers in vibrant blue,
Each petal speaking his love for you."

Candles in the Rain

Kathy's 27th Birthday

"Your father rose, voice calm yet true,
You would be twenty-seven; this walk's for you.

I pulled the candles from my pack,
Still dry and safe despite the track.
An orange stood where cake should be,
A symbol born from memory."

Kathy's 27 Birthday Candles

Forever Her Mimi

"Tiny fingers reached out, and without any plan,
She planted herself right next to where I began.
Her soft voice like music, her giggles like art,
And in that one moment, she captured my heart.

I watched her grow, year after year,
A light in my life, a soul pure and clear."

"The pain in my heart will always search for her"
- Michelle Boodoo

A String of Beads

"Now it rests upon my chest,
A priceless treasure, love confessed.
Each bead, a little heart, a story told,
A symbol of her love, worth more than gold."

A Pilgrimage for Kathy

Walking the Camino de Santiago

"Beneath the rising sun,
We walked the path you never got to run.
Hundreds of miles beneath a sky so wide,
Through valleys and hills, with you as our guide.

From France to Spain, step after step,
Carrying your love and the tears we've wept."

Walking for Kathy 🖤

A Blanket of Love

"Wrapped in warmth, each night's embrace,
A piece of me in every knitted space.
You said it felt just like my hug,
A steady, soft, unending tug."

KATHY'S

BLANKET

Flowers For Kathy

"Each week, I gather flowers with care,
From garden paths and morning air.
A ritual soft, a sacred chore,
For the one I'll miss forevermore."

"I etched your name upon my skin,
A quiet mark, a voice within.
Your initials, bold and true,
A semicolon, meaning too."

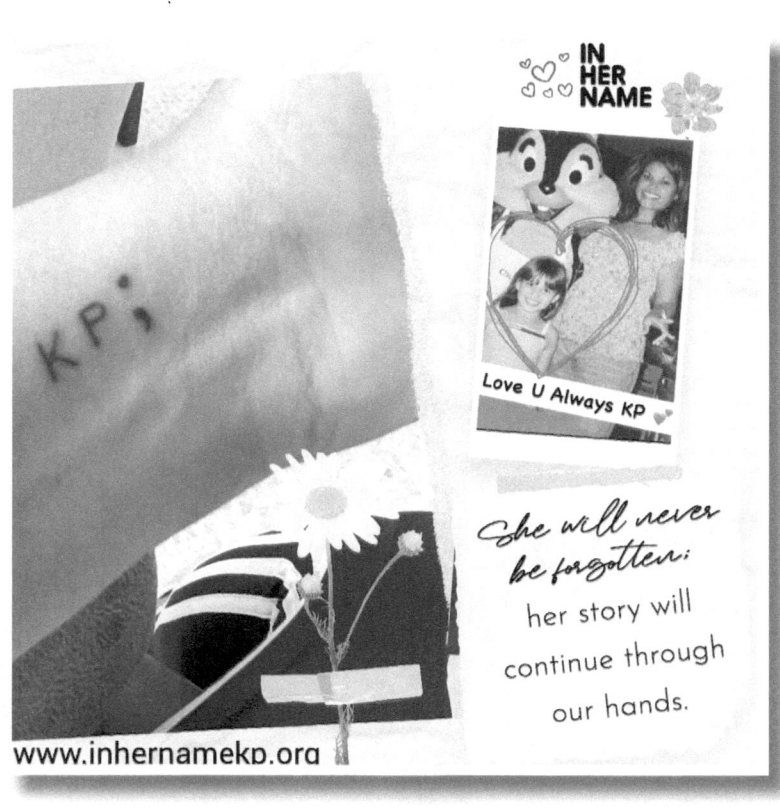

She will never be forgotten; her story will continue through our hands.

www.inhernamekp.org

A Degree

"Your name engraved, your journey told,
A paper crowned in heartfelt gold.
The school had given more than they knew,
A piece of your dream, now alive and true."

YOUR REFLECTIONS

Name of Poem:
Page #

_____

_____

_____

_____

_____

_____

_____

_____

_____

_____

Epilogue

Dr. Boodoo is committed to her work at *In Her Name* to support people who are struggling with their mental health, just as Kathy once did. She also plans to create future collections of poems focused on mental health, depression, and suicide prevention, offering words of comfort and hope to others.

While Dr. Boodoo doesn't know exactly where this new purpose will lead, she finds strength in the belief that Kathy's love and essence remain beside her, and that love is her guide, her light, and her reason to keep going.

She hopes that these words not only honor Kathy's memory but also bring comfort to others who are grieving. May you find in these pages the love and strength that come from carrying the memory of those your heart grieves for.

Acknowledgement

I am deeply grateful to Santiago Perez for his love, strength, and unwavering support. Throughout this journey of grief and remembrance, he has been a pillar of resilience, helping to carry the weight of sorrow for our beloved Kathy. This book is as much a reflection of his love and devotion to honor Kathy as it is of mine, and I am sincerely thankful for the ways Santiago has encouraged and sustained me in bringing these words to life.

Santiago Perez is Kathy's dad.

Cover Photo Story

Cover Photo Credit: Dr. Boodoo

I would like to share the story behind the photo on the cover of this book. Photography has always been one of my passions, and I often found myself taking countless pictures of Kathy and of anything that caught my eye.

In the winter of 2017, Kathy and I were sitting in the back seat of a car, heading out for the day. The sky looked so breathtakingly beautiful that I pulled out my phone to snap a picture. The photo automatically uploaded to Dropbox, and in time, I completely forgot about it.

When Kathy passed away in 2022, my world stopped. In the first few days, I found myself asking again and again, *Where are you, Kathy? Where are you?* I was in shock, clinging to anything that might bring my Kathy back.

About a week later, I had to gather photos of Kathy for the funeral home. That night, I opened Dropbox and began moving her pictures into a new folder. As I quietly worked, the same question echoed in my heart: *Kathy, where are you?*

Just then, the very next image that appeared on my screen was the forgotten sky photo from 2017. The clouds looked picture-perfect, but what took my breath away was the reflection faintly visible within them: Kathy's face.

In that moment, I knew exactly where she was.

Photo of the Author

The first photo shows Kathy and me hiking in California. In the second, I'm wearing the necklace from the poem, *A String of Beads*.

About the Author

Dr. Michelle V. Boodoo is the CEO and Founder of *In Her Name*, an organization dedicated to promoting positive mental health and preventing suicide. She earned her Ph.D. in Education and has spent much of her professional career working in higher education. Her passion for that field was always clear: helping students pursue their educational dreams. Her last role at a university was as Vice President of Student Financial Services, where she oversaw financial aid departments across multiple campuses.

In April 2022, Dr. Boodoo's life changed forever when she lost her beloved stepdaughter, Kathy, to suicide. This devastating loss brought her to a crossroads, forcing her to reevaluate her purpose and life's direction. Just months later, she founded *In Her Name* to honor Kathy's memory and to provide hope, resources, and support for individuals and families navigating the challenges of mental health, including depression, social anxiety, bullying, and suicide prevention.

Through *In Her Name*, Dr. Boodoo found a way to channel her grief into meaningful work, but she also longed for something more personal and tangible. Writing became that outlet. She began documenting memories of Kathy's special moments, birthdays, and holidays, as well as the raw emotions of grief itself. From those writings, this collection of poems was born. It is both a tribute to Kathy and a source of comfort for others who are grieving.

Today, Dr. Boodoo continues to walk this new path with pain and purpose. Guided by Kathy's love and essence, she is committed to making a difference in the lives of those impacted by mental health struggles ... until the day she and Kathy are reunited again.

Contact Information for Author

Dr. Michelle V. Boodoo
Website: www.inhernamekp.org
Email: Michelle@inhernamekp.org
Instagram: https://www.instagram.com/inhernamekp
Facebook: https://www.facebook.com/michelle.boodoo.1